To Hades and Heaven

Johannes Tertsunen

To Hades and Heaven

English translation:

Ester Carreon

Cover art:

MJT

Scripture taken from:

King James Bible (1679),
Old Testament.

New American Standard Edition (1901),
New Testament.

ISBN 978-952-93-1675-5 (paperback)
ISBN 978-952-93-1676-2 (PDF)

"I see many books, I see you writing.

You think you´re not able to do it, but you are, Holy Spirit is able."

M.L

"I see a book that has been written, you begin to write it, you begin to write exactly what is needed to be written.

You know certain things, that the Lord your God has given for you, and when you do it, it will bring great joy to others."

M.L

Martta Carita

The unexpected experience

Many have had the experience of receiving a phone call that changes the day. This also happened to me on a beautiful Sunday morning in early October, 2000.

Our 20-year-old daughter's partner called, telling us that our daughter had killed herself.

Our daughter had been drinking in a restaurant the night before, where there also was the ex-wife of her partner. That caused a fight between them, that continued later at night in their apartment. On morning, she was found hanging from end of bedsheet, the other end was tied to the attachment of the ceiling lamp. Her spouse, who had been sleeping on the sofa, saw her on the floor, strangled with the sheet.

In the autopsy, the authorities wrote that the immediate cause of death was by hanging, and the autopsy also had the note "use of alcohol", the blood alcohol content being 0,15 %. The autopsy also stated, that her left temple, and the left and right side of the back of her head were bruised, and that she had a small bruise on her upper lip. Her partner told that he gave a small slap on her face.

She would have turned 21 in a month. My older brother, who was one year older than me, died in the same way, when he would have turned 21 the next day. Also, my uncle died in the war, when he was 21 years old.

I knew my daughter died in sin, and that brought me the knowledge how I couldn't save my daughter, even when I had been living in communion with God.

Our daughter had been a believer when she was younger, but by teenage years she got involved with bad company, and followed by that, to the life of sin.

The concern for our daughter's eternal fate filled my heart, and I left outside driving aimlessly around with my car, since it was the place where I often prayed, and where God often spoke to me. I was driving around awhile, and the only words that I told to God were: "Why didn't you tell me anything?", because I was thinking, that if God had revealed beforehand the approaching danger, we could have changed it through prayer.

My anguish was beyond words, and my only hope to change what had happened, was to raise our daughter from the dead. The most important thing for me - in the lives of my close ones and in my own life - is that they have eternal life. Everything else, be it however good, felt meaningless beside it.

I returned home, and I thought about calling to Juennine Fox, whom we had met earlier. She told earlier, that God had told her to raise the dead.

So I called to the home where she was staying at the time, and when I told her what had happened, she promised to call back after she first asked God about this. When she called back, I gave the phone to my wife, since she spoke better English, and so began the miraculous experience.

I was sitting in the livingroom, and peace filled my whole being, a supernatural joy flowed into my heart.

Juennine told my wife, how God had strongly

7

talked to her when she had entered in prayer. God had told her: "I can't break the promise I have given to this woman".

I didn't know that my wife had received a special promise while traveling in Israel. She was sitting in a café, and a woman prophesied over her life and told her, that God will save all her children and the whole family.

When my wife and Juennine were praying together on the phone, Juennine saw an open vision: The lightning of God hit a great gate and the gate opened. Our daughter rose up from there to meet Jesus Christ, and Jesus took her into His arms.

I know that there is people who cannot believe that you can pray for the dead, I don't recommend that anyone takes the risk and dies unsaved, but the fact is, that some have done this and have been saved, even when they have already left their bodies. Some have returned back from dead to tell about it, but not all.

On that same Sunday, there was a meeting in Kerava City-church, where Juennine was the visiting speaker. She first shared the amazing things that happened on that morning. I have written here the first part of the sermon as it was spoken that day:

Juennine Fox

"I wanted to start off with a testimony, and I know it's a testimony because I know by the Spirit, amen. It didn't start off as a testimony, but this morning I received a phone call, it was a phone call from someone whom I didn't get the chance to know very well, but someone who I loved because I saw her in one of my meetings. They told the matter to Ellu, and she was very concerned, and she ran to tell me the matter, and told me that, one of the ladies who had been in one of my services, had just heard a report that her daughter had hang herself.

Now that's not a good testimony at all, we want to give our comfort to her, and just let her know that we love her. It was very hard for me to take it. First when I heard the news, I was almost paralyzed, I'm sure just as she was. The message to me was, would I pray. Of course that's all we can do is to pray. But as I started to pray, I said: "Lord, I really ask you to speak to me, how do I comfort her? Because her daughter is dead, and she's waiting for me to call her back, and I don't want to speak any word but Your word".

So I got very quiet and said: "Holy Spirit, I ask you really to speak to me, give me Your word".

Now before I finish telling you the rest of this story, God has used me three times to pray for the people who have been raised from the dead, so I have faith. I know God can raise the dead, because His word says He is the resurrection and He is the life. That even though if we 're dead, if we believe, yet shall we live. He who lives and believes in Jesus Christ shall never die. He is the resurrection and life, and He holds the keys to Hell and death, even now Jesus Christ holds the keys.

So the truth that each and every one of us must die is the reality, that we all must leave this earth soon and die in this natural realm. But the truth is also, that we really never really die, we live eternally somewhere. Either for eternity in Hell or eternity with Jesus Christ.

I'm going to talk about a very sensitive issue today, because we got some victory this morning. And the Lord said: "I want you to speak this message to my church, that I have the keys of Hell and of death". And

many times we have given up in the face of
death, when we heard that a loved one has
died. If they did not serve Jesus Christ, we
think that there's no hope, there's no hope.

But as I went into my closet to seek a word
from the Lord, the Holy Spirit spoke to me
almost audibly, and He said: "Juennine, My
mercy endures forever, My mercy endures
forever, My mercy endures forever". I said:
"Well Lord, how can I give her this word that
"Your mercy endures forever", because her
daughter hang herself, that was suicide. And
we don't really believe that she received
Jesus Christ as her saviour". But immediatly
I was quickened, it was like a lightning bolt
went through my spirit and God spoke to me.

And He said: "She died a few hours ago,
who said it's too late? What's the difference
between heaven time and earth time? Who
said it's too late? I AM the one who holds the
keys to Hell and death. I AM life, I AM the
author of life, and you have a relationship
with Me. I've given you authority, I've spoken
to you in My word, that the purpose of your
life is to raise the dead. Freely I have given

to you, now freely give to others".
And there was a faith that rose up in my heart, and the Holy Spirit started to give me instructions of exactly what to do. And He showed me, that there had been a curse on the family, because another person in the family had died because of suicide as well. And He said: "I have given you the power to remit sins, to forgive them, to release them and to retain them". And this is not only for me, but this is for every child of God who claims to be a christian, who walks according to the commandments of Jesus Christ. You know that Scripture is not in the Bible for us just to ignore, I have ignored it most of my life. It says: "Whoever's sins you forgive, they are forgiven". Which means, release, they're released. And whoever's sins you retain, hold onto, you hold onto them. And the Spirit of Counsel started to speak so specific, as if Jesus Christ was standing next to me, and giving me line by line the order what He wanted me to do.

The Keys

He said: "Right now, this child is in the chambers of death, but I'm going to give you the keys to get to bring her up now". And so He told me first to forgive her sins, to release her into the forgiveness of Jesus Christ. No, I cannot forgive anyone's sins, but two thousand years ago Jesus already did, and I'm only proclaiming what He already did two thousand years ago. So the truth of the matter is, your sins have been forgiven.

And then He said: "I want you to go back, and I want you to release the generations from that curse of suicide, and forgive all the generations, all for since. And break the curse of death and suicide, that took her life in the first place". And I broke the curse of death and suicide.

And we called her on the phone, and I said: "I received a word from the Lord, that Jesus Christ is going to receive your daughter, we're going to command her to come out of Hell.

And I believe Jesus Christ is going to receive her in heaven, that her spirit is going to travel.
I believe Jesus Christ is going to take her soul from Hell, and receive her unto Himself. Because He has given me a commandment, and He said that it's not too late, she's still in hours of mercy, and He will receive her".
And then He gave me one more promise, He said: "I have given her promise".
He said: "I am not a liar, and My promise to her is, that her and her household shall be saved. So I'm going to be true according to My word, and you are to speak that promise, that I promised her that I was going to save every child".

So I said: "Lord, I have to do this". I called her on the phone, we started to pray. I said: "I've never done this before, this goes beyond anything in my mind. But the Lord has spoken to me, and I've never experienced this in my life". But as we started to pray, and I started to speak, the power of God came over that phone. And I commanded her spirit.

I said: "Come forth!". And the Lord said: "You are to tell her to come to the kingdom of God, you are to bring her to the kingdom of God". And I called her spirit forth to the kingdom of God, because the Lord did not tell me He was going to raise her here, He said: "I'm going to raise her there, I'm going to put her in my arms right now".

Open vision

And I actually had an open vision, where I saw so clearly, I saw her being lifted from the gates of Hell, and I saw a light, as if lightning started to strike Hell, and there was a big light that hit the gates of Hell. And the arms of Jesus reached down, and took her soul and lifted her right up.

And at the same time while I'm praying, she saw the same vision. The exact same vision of just two arms reaching down and getting her, the arms of Jesus, and Him comforting her. And I saw her spirit just being hugged by the Lord Jesus Christ. And she was saved.

From the time that prayer finished, there was a peace that passes all understanding, that no human being on earth can give a person who's grieving. Peace can only come from the Holy Ghost. And I'm sure those of you who have lost loved ones, you know it only can be God's peace that comforts you in a moment like that. I received such a joy in my spirit, I knew that I knew that I knew it had been done. I had a witness that she saw the same thing, she knew it was done. On the other end, the lady who had the problem, that was her daughter, she also received the comfort of God, the mother received the comfort of God. Immediatly there was silence and just a peace beyond imaginable.

And within 7 minutes I received a phone call again from her husband, laughing, going: "Ahahaha! I'm so happy! I'm so happy!".

Only the Spirit of God can touch you and give you joy. When you find out your child has just taken their life, only the Spirit of God can comfort us and give us joy. The Bible says: "The kingdom of God is righteousness, peace and joy". And I asked for a sign, that the Lord would comfort them, and give them a knowing that she was okay.

And I wanted just exhort us tonight, and encourage you tonight, that God has given us the keys of Hell and death, because He has the keys. And not to always just give up, when we find out someone is dead.

The Lord reminded me, He said: "I told you to raise the dead. I didn't ask you whether they were saved or if they were not saved, I said raise the dead". I encourage you to have hope, that if you have been praying for a loved one who died prematurely, and you gave them to the Lord, that God doesn't lose His children, that He is faithful to keep that which we entrusted to Him."
(Here ends the speech of Juennine Fox.)

Not many preachers would go, do or say something, that doesn't really go with the common view of things, so God had chosen a woman beforehand, whom He could use for this purpose.

Juennine was not supposed to come to Finland, but God knew beforehand what would happen. God spoke to the person who was supposed to come to Finland to preach, that he shouldn't go, but that he should ask Juennine to go instead of him.

A few days before our daughter died, we was in a home meeting where Juennine was speaking, and my wife experienced a strange phenomenon.

In 1977, our firstborn died in her womb when she was 8 months pregnant, and my wife had to give birth to him because he was a fully developed baby. We had been married for over a year, and this was quite a shocking experience for us, and I couldn't understand it. But then my wife experienced this wonderful presence of "the power of Jesus' resurrection", that she had never felt before and not after that, until in the home meeting, where Juennine was speaking. It was like a foreshadowing of what was going to happen few days later.

That Wednesday, before the Sunday when our daughter passed away, we were visiting our daughter Martta. When we were about to leave, I was sitting in the driver's seat in the 9-person car in the parking lot, and these words came to my heart:

"Go tell your daughter Martta, that she will always be your daughter, that you love her and that she's always welcome home".

It was a strong feeling, but I was thinking that I could go back later, that I shouldn't keep people waiting in the car. So I decided to tell it to her another time, "there's always

21

time" I though, but there was no "another time".

I'm writing this, that no one else will make the same mistake as I did, but rather listens to God or his heart, if something like this happens.

Few weeks after the funeral, I was watching a tv-program called "To Hell and Back" from the christian satellite channel TBN. People shared their experience of what had happened to them when they had died. When Howard Storm told in the program: "I believe one of the reasons why God gave me this experience, is that I can share it with someone. I never know with whom...".

I knew I was one of the people who was meant to hear his testimony.

Howard told how he had died, left his body and went to his horrible place, but then a children's song came to his mind, "Jesus loves me", which led him to turn to God and he shouted in the darkness: "Please Jesus, save me!".

And so can you also call to God. The Bible tells us:

for, **Whosoever** *shall call upon the name of the Lord shall be saved.* *(Rom 10:13)*

Some may say, that it's useless to pray for people who have already died, but who is to put the limit? Everything is possible for him who believes!

*Jesus looking upon them saith, With men it is impossible, but not with God: for **all things are possible with God**.*
(Mark 10:27)

Jesus preached in the underworld:

Because Christ also suffered for sins once, the righteous for the unrighteous, that he might bring us to God; being put to death in the flesh, but made alive in the spirit;
(1.Pet 3:18)

*in which also he went and **preached unto the spirits in prison**, (1.Pet 3:19)*

that aforetime were disobedient, when the longsuffering of God waited in the days of Noah, while the ark was a preparing, wherein few, that is, eight souls, were saved through water: (1.Pet 3:20)

The Curse

One of my ancestors was a known sorcerer, who was at least one of the channels for the curse in the family line.

However, curses won't affect those who have moved from the kingdom of darkness to the kingdom of light. But if a believer goes to the kingdom of darkness, in other words abandons God and goes to the life of sin, he is under the laws of darkness (one of them being curses), as happened to our daughter.

By staying in the kingdom of light, living in communion with God, one is free from all the curses, being in the shelter of the Most High. The curses of darkness can be broken, so that those who are not yet in the kingdom of God, can be free from them through intercession.

*to open their eyes, that they may turn from darkness to light and **from the power of Satan unto God**, that they may receive remission of sins and an inheritance among them that are sanctified by faith in me. (Act 26:18)*

My earlier experience of sorrow turning into peace

Finally, I will tell you about my experience, about how one can receive tremendous comfort in sorrow.

I was 16, when my beloved mother died in car accident at age 45, and the word sorrow doesn't even justify how I felt.

I didn't know that my mother was so dear to me, until she passed away suddenly. She was the dearest person to me, and therefore my sorrow was beyond depth, as nothing could comfort me.

Three years later, I came to communion with God through Jesus Christ. I had a concrete experience of the power of the Holy Spirit, I was truly happy.

Then a month after, my older brother hang himself, and when I got to know that, I walked into a forest and kneeled down to pray. Then it happened, like an invisible cloud had surrounded me, a great peace was overflowing into my being, and I heard the words:

"I UNDERSTAND". The God of comfort told just these two words, and I knew He perfectly understood what I was feeling.

When I got up, everything looked so beautiful: the sky, and then the birds were singing as if to me, and I had great peace and rest, thank God.

You will receive a great help, when you kneel before the God of comfort, He is the only one who really knows you inside out, and He loves you.

Part 2

Information about afterlife in God's word

"God is a Spirit" (Joh 4:24)

When your body dies, it turns into dust.

"till thou return unto the ground; for out of it wast thou taken: for dust thou art, and unto dust shalt thou return." (Gen 3:19)"

The body is often described as a dwelling place, or as an earthly house from which we move out, or after it we put on a new cloth.

*For we know that if **the earthly house** of our tabernacle be dissolved, we have a building from God, a house not made with hands, eternal, in the heavens. (2.Col 5:1)*

For verily in this we groan, longing to be clothed upon with our habitation which is from heaven: (2.Col 5:2)

if so be that being clothed we shall not be found naked. (2.Col 5:3)

What then happens to our spirit and soul when our body dies?

Where do they go to, is there any information, and if there is, how do I know it's real?

You can have the information from people who have left their body by death or through another event, but those are just different experiences. The facts we can read from what God has declared to us, therefore we read those first, and in the light of them we can study the experiences of others.

King Saul and the witch of Endor

Now Samuel was dead, and all Israel had lamented him, and buried him in Ramah, even in his own city. And Saul had put away those that had familiar spirits, and the wizards, out of the land. (1.Sam 28:3)

And the Philistines gathered themselves together, and came and pitched in Shunem: and Saul gathered all Israel together, and they pitched in Gilboa. (1.Sam 28:4)

And when Saul saw the host of the Philistines, he was afraid, and his heart greatly trembled. (1.Sam 28:5)

And when Saul enquired of the LORD, the LORD answered him not, neither by dreams, nor by Urim, nor by prophets. (1.Sam 28:6)

Then said Saul unto his servants, Seek me a woman that hath a familiar spirit, that I may go to her, and enquire of her. And his servants said to him, Behold, there is a woman that hath a familiar spirit at Endor. (1.Sam 28:7)

And Saul disguised himself, and put on other raiment, and he went, and two men with him, and they came to the woman by night: and he said, I pray thee, divine unto me by the familiar spirit, and bring me him up, whom I shall name unto thee. (1.Sam 28:8)

And the woman said unto him, Behold, thou knowest what Saul hath done, how he hath cut off those that have familiar spirits, and the wizards, out of the land: wherefore then layest thou a snare for my life, to cause me to die? (1.Sam 28:9)

And Saul sware to her by the LORD, saying, As the LORD liveth, there shall no punishment happen to thee for this thing. (1.Sam 28:10)

Then said the woman, Whom shall I bring up unto thee? And he said, Bring me up Samuel. (1.Sam 28:11)

And when the woman saw Samuel, she cried with a loud voice: and the woman spake to Saul, saying, Why hast thou deceived me? for thou art Saul. (1.Sam 28:12)

And the king said unto her, Be not afraid: for what sawest thou? And the woman said unto

Saul, I saw gods ascending out of the earth. (1.Sam 28:13)

And he said unto her, What form is he of? And she said, An old man cometh up; and he is covered with a mantle. And Saul perceived that it was Samuel, and he stooped with his face to the ground, and bowed himself. (1.Sam 28:14)

And Samuel said to Saul, Why hast thou disquieted me, *to bring me up? And Saul answered, I am sore distressed; for the Philistines make war against me, and God is departed from me, and answereth me no more, neither by prophets, nor by dreams: therefore I have called thee, that thou mayest make known unto me what I shall do. (1.Sam 28:15)*

Then said Samuel, Wherefore then dost thou ask of me, seeing the LORD is departed from thee, and is become thine enemy? (1.Sam 28:16)

And the LORD hath done to him, as he spake by me: for the LORD hath rent the kingdom out of thine hand, and given it to thy neighbour, even to David: (1.Sam 28:17)

Because thou obeyedst not the voice of the LORD, nor executedst his fierce wrath upon Amalek, therefore hath the LORD done this thing unto thee this day. (1.Sam 28:18)

*Moreover the LORD will also deliver Israel with thee into the hand of the Philistines: and **to morrow shalt thou and thy sons be with me**: the LORD also shall deliver the host of Israel into the hand of the Philistines. (1.Sam 28:19)*

So Saul died for his transgression which he committed against the LORD, even against the word of the LORD, which he kept not, and also for asking counsel of one that had a familiar spirit, to enquire of it; (1.Chro 10:13)

This story in the Bible illuminates well the state of the dead, as prophet Samuel's words "Why hast thou disquieted me, to bring me up?" tell us, that Samuel is well in the underworld, where the familiar spirit had access to. By this, we can understand better Jesus' story of the rich man and Lazarus.

The rich man and Lazarus

Now there was a certain rich man, and he was clothed in purple and fine linen, faring sumptuously every day: (Luk 16:19)

and a certain beggar named Lazarus was laid at his gate, full of sores, (Luk 16:20)

and desiring to be fed with the crumbs that fell from the rich man's table; yea, even the dogs came and licked his sores. (Luk 16:21)

And it came to pass, that the beggar died, and that he was carried away by the angels into Abraham's bosom: and the rich man also died, and was buried. (Luk 16:22)

*And in **Hades** he lifted up his eyes, being in torments, and seeth Abraham afar off, and Lazarus in his bosom. (Luk 16:23)*

And he cried and said, Father Abraham, have mercy on me, and send Lazarus, that he may dip the tip of his finger in water, and cool my tongue; for I am in anguish in this flame. (Luk 16:24)

But Abraham said, Son, remember that thou

in thy lifetime receivedst thy good things, and Lazarus in like manner evil things: but now here he is comforted, and thou art in anguish. (Luk 16:25)

*And besides all this, between us and you **there is a great gulf fixed**, that they that would pass from hence to you may not be able, and that none may cross over from thence to us. (Luk 16:26)*

And he said, I pray thee therefore, father, that thou wouldest send him to my father's house; (Luk 16:27)

for I have five brethren; that he may testify unto them, lest they also come into this place of torment. (Luk 16:28)

But Abraham saith, They have Moses and the prophets; let them hear them.(Luk 16:29)

And he said, Nay, father Abraham: but if one go to them from the dead, they will repent. (Luk 16:30)

And he said unto him, If they hear not Moses and the prophets, neither will they be persuaded, if one rise from the dead. (Luk 16:31)

Jesus told about a great gulf that separated people from each others. The underworld is a place inside earth, that also has valleys and different departments, where people went when they died, except Elijah and Enoch, whom God took directly to heaven. Also God Himself "buried" Moses.

And all this changed, when Jesus died and went down to underworld to free those who were captives in there, and took them with him to the third heaven, to the paradise beyond space.

Here are few Bible verses concerning this topic.

Underworld

In these and in many other parts of the Finnish translation of the Bible, the word *Hell* has been translated as *Hades*, and Hades is a greek word meaning "*the world of the dead*", translated also as *Hell, grave, pit.*

(In Hebrew=sheh-olé, sheh-olé.)

And it came to pass, as he had made an end of speaking all these words, that the ground clave asunder that was under them: (Num 16:31)

And the earth opened her mouth, and swallowed them up, and their houses, and all the men that appertained unto Korah, and all their goods. (Num 16:32)

*They, and all that appertained to them, **went down alive into the pit**, (sheh-olé ,sheh-olé) and the earth closed upon them: and they perished from among the congregation. (Num 16:33)*

*The LORD killeth, and maketh alive: he bringeth down to the **grave**,(sheh-olé ,sheh-olé) and bringeth up. (1.Sam 2:6)*

*Her (an adulterous woman) house is the way to Hell (sheh-olé ,sheh-olé), **going down to the chambers of death**. (Pro 7:27)*

*But he knoweth not that the dead are there; and that **her** (an adulterous woman) **guests are in the depths of Hell** (sheh-olé ,sheh-olé). (Pro 9:18)*

The clearing of the underworld

The following verses tell us, how Jesus, after dying on the cross, went to the underworld and took some of those who were in there, to the third heaven, to paradise.

and the Living one; and I was dead, and behold, I am alive for evermore, and I have **the keys of death and of Hades.** *(Rev 1:18)*

Wherefore he saith, When he ascended on high, he led **captivity captive**, *And gave gifts unto men. (Eph 4:8)*

(Now this, He ascended, what is it but that he also descended into the **lower parts of the earth?** *(Eph 4:9)*

He that descended is the same also that ascended far above all the heavens, that he might fill all things.) (Eph 4:10)

And he said unto him, Verily I say unto thee, **Today** *shalt thou be* **with me in Paradise**. *(Luk 23:43)*

So Jesus promised to him, that he doesn't have to go to the underworld, but he can go with Him to the third heaven, and so it happened.

Nowadays this happens to everyone who dies and believes in Jesus Christ.
They go straight to the third heaven, to paradise.

*I know a man in Christ, fourteen years ago (whether in the body, I know not; or whether out of the body, I know not; God knoweth), such a one **caught up even to the third heaven.** (2 Co 12:2)*

And I know such a man (whether in the body, or apart from the body, I know not; God knoweth), (2 Co 12:3)

*how that he was **caught up into Paradise**, and heard unspeakable words, which it is not lawful for a man to utter. (2 Co 12:4)*

Many have no clear concept of the difference of underworld and Hell, especially not in the English speaking world, where the word *underworld (Hades)* has been translated as *Hell*.

In the future, some years from now, **the first people, the antichrist and the false prophet go to Hell.** Antichrist (the beast) is captured, when Jesus returns to earth from heaven, and brings peace on earth for one thousand years. This happens in near future, in the beginning of the kingdom of one thousand years of peace.

*And the beast was taken, and with him the false prophet that wrought the signs in his sight, wherewith he deceived them that had received the mark of the beast and them that worshipped his image: they two were **cast alive into the lake of fire** that burneth with brimstone: (Rev 19:20)*

Later, after one thousand years, we see them still in the lake of fire, where the devil is also thrown in the end of the one-thousand-year-kingdom.

After the last judgement, death, underworld and the people who´s name is not in the book of life, will be also thrown to the lake of fire.

*And the devil that deceived them was **cast into the lake of fire** and brimstone, **where*** *are also the beast and the false prophet; and they shall be tormented day and night for ever and ever. (Rev 20:10)*

So when a person dies, he goes to the paradise in third heaven if he believes in Jesus Christ, but otherwise he goes to the underworld, to wait over a thousand years for the day of judgement, when also all the others who have passed away, will be judged.

And I saw a great white throne, and him that sat upon it, from whose face the earth and the heaven fled away; and there was found no place for them. (Rev 20:11)

*And **I saw the dead**, the great and the small, standing before the throne; and books were opened: and another book was opened, which is the book of life: and the dead were judged out of the things which were written in the books, according to their works. (Rev 20:12)*

*And the sea gave up the dead that were in it; and **death and Hades** gave up the dead that were in them: and they were judged every man according to their works*

(Rev 20:13)

*And **death and Hades were cast into the lake of fire**. This is the second death, even the lake of fire. (Rev 20:14)*

*And if any was not found written in the book of life, he was **cast into the lake of fire**. (Rev 20:15)*

(Rev 6:8) and (Rev 20:14) tell us that Hades and death are not only places: *"death and Hades were **cast into the lake of fire**".*

*Jesus said: And if thy hand or thy foot causeth thee to stumble, cut it off, and cast it from thee: it is good for thee to enter into life maimed or halt, rather than having two hands or two feet to be **cast into the eternal fire**. (Mat 18:8)*

*And if thine eye causeth thee to stumble, pluck it out, and cast it from thee: it is good for thee to enter into life with one eye, rather than having two eyes to be **cast into the Hell of fire**. (Mat 18:9)*

*And from there we understand that Hell (Geenna in greece) is a lake of fire, the only place where there is **everlasting** fire.*

The most important thing in your life

You´re truly "lucky", because you have heard of eternal life and about receiving it, which you can do right now. The good news have reached you now! Jesus Christ was cruelly killed, that you might be saved.
Christ died for our sins according to the scriptures; (1Co 15:3)

So by praying this prayer now, you can receive the forgiveness of your sins, eternal life through Jesus Christ, say to God now:

Almighty God, the Creator of heaven and earth, I want to believe that Jesus Christ has died for my sins, I want to have eternal life and do Your will in my life. Therefore I ask, forgive all my sins, Jesus Christ come to my heart and be the Lord of my life, here and now. Thank You for the salvation, thank you Jesus Christ, thank you.

Let me also have the gift of the Holy Spirit, thank you.

Thank you, thank you, thank you, thank you, thank you, thank you...

... abounding in thanksgiving. (Col 2:7)

Jesus Christ said:

And I say unto you, Ask, and it shall be given you; seek, and ye shall find; knock, and it shall be opened unto you. (Luk 11:9)

*For **every one** that asketh receiveth; and he that seeketh findeth; and to him that knocketh it shall be opened.
(Luk 11:10)*

And of which of you that is a father shall his son ask a loaf, and he give him a stone? or a fish, and he for a fish give him a serpent? (Luk 11:11)

Or if he shall ask an egg, will he give him a scorpion? (Luk 11:12)

*If ye then, being evil, know how to give good gifts unto your children, how much more shall your **heavenly Father give the Holy Spirit to them that ask him?** (Luk 11:13)*

It's highly important, that you ask Jesus Christ to baptize you in Holy Spirit, so that you can pray everyday in Holy Spirit, because that is one of the greatest resources and helps to this life.

Now that you have received Jesus Christ, you have been made perfect forever, before God.

*For by one offering he hath **perfected** for **ever** them that are sanctified. (Heb 10:14)*

This great verse tells you, that you have been made perfect forever, so that you can never become more perfect, and you can never attain a better position before God than you already have. You can't add anything to perfectness, you are perfectly righteous, as righteous as Jesus Christ.

***Being therefore justified by faith**, we have peace with God through our Lord Jesus Christ;(Rom 5:1)*

*through whom also we have had our access by faith into this grace **wherein we stand**; and we rejoice in hope of the glory of God. (Rom 5:2)*

Therefore when you receive Jesus Christ, you also receive His righteousness, as He received your sins when He was on the cross.

You have been given righteousness as a gift, which is perfect righteousness, **so that no one in the whole world is more righteous than you.**

*By one offering Jesus Christ had **perfected*** - so for how long time? FOREVER, which means unending time, eternity.

Jesus Christ, with His sacrifice at Golgotha, has made you perfect for the rest of your life and beyond.

***for all have sinned**, and fall short of the glory of God; (Rom 3:23)*

***being justified freely by his grace** through the redemption that is in Christ Jesus: (Rom 3:24)*

The biggest gift you have ever received is righteousness, it's given as a 100% gift, and inside it's 100% gift too.

*For the wages of sin is death; **but the free gift of God is eternal life** in Christ Jesus our Lord. (Rom 6:23)*

Last resort-prayer

(By last resort-prayer I mean, that no one should leave their eternal fate depending on a last resort.)

However,

if it so happens that you die, and you realize that you have already left your body, if you haven't made the decision while living here on earth, then at the latest turn to Jesus Christ and ask Him to save you.

Howard Storm cried out to God to save him, and even when he did this when he had already died, he got saved. He died as an atheist, but had heard about Jesus when he was a child. It's much surer to receive now the gift of salvation, because now it's 100% sure.

*(for he saith, At an acceptable time I hearkened unto thee, And in a day of salvation did I succor thee: **behold, now is the acceptable time; behold, now is the day of salvation**): (2.Col 6:2)*

Eternal life

When I received faith, I was excited that I had come in communion with God, that Jesus had given me a supernatural peace and had set me free from addictions and all that is evil, my life had turned good.

But salvation is something much bigger than just the salvation of this life, this life lasts just 100 years, and after that begins those millions of years that the salvation is concerned about.

*If we have **only** hoped in Christ in **this life**, we are of all men most pitiable.*
(1Co 15:19)

*For God so loved the world, that he gave his only begotten Son, that whosoever believeth on him should not perish, but have **eternal life**. (Joh 3:16)*

The Red Cross and other charity organizations do a great job bringing help to people, but they can't bring the most important help that a person needs, it can only be made by the church, only we can bring eternal life to people.

The greatest good deed is to give your fellowman eternal life, nothing compares to the gift of eternal life, which actually every believer can give to his fellowman.

Jesus answered and said unto her, Every one that drinketh of this water shall thirst again: (Joh 4:13)

*but whosoever drinketh of the water that I shall give him shall never thirst; but the water that I shall give him **shall become in him a well of water springing up unto eternal life.** (Joh 4:14)*

Look at the heavens and think, how far into the space a man can travel before it ends, and when does time end?

Thus millions, millions and millions....years...continue...continue...

What a wonderful future is ahead of us, and we can only understand a mere glimmer of it when we read the Bible.

Only in the Bible are the words of everlasting life, I wish everyone could have a Bible.

And finally, an important guideline in life:

Read the bible diligently, and visit the meetings of a living church.

Free Bible in English and in many other languages:

www.e-sword.net

If you have something you'd like to ask, please send email to:

question@armo.info

Thank you.
Johannes